Rapture

Fact or Fiction

You Decide

*

Is Christ not risen?

This is the third in   The Book Series to Consider

All scripture taken from King James Companion Bible 1611 with Structures and Critical, Explanatory and Suggestive Notes and with 198 Appendixes

Although not endorsed by Shepherd's Chapel references made are with permission.

Copyrighted material is Used by permission of Thomas Nelson Inc.

Copyrighted material is Used by permission of Random House Inc.

Printed in the United States of America

ISBN 978-0-9777851-4-8   this book

ISBN 978-0-9777851-6-2   four biblical book set

Coming soon   www.publishinggodsway.com

To contact us   publishinggodsway@bv.net   or
                     352-391-1959

THERE IS NO GREATER GIFT THAN THE TRUTHFUL WORD OF GOD

My gift to you

Occasion

From

Date

Dedication

This work is dedicated to all of God's children who have been "caught up" in man's whirlwind of confusion, lies and deception regarding religion, theology and Christianity!

This work is dedicated to all who have either left the church or those who don't believe in church but never knew why!

This work is dedicated to those who say they don't believe in God, when in fact, they only say this because they don't know what to believe with the creation of all the church denominations!

This work is dedicated to all who are worshiping in churches that are not of God, but sadly they do not know the difference between false doctrine and God's doctrine!

This work is dedicated to the lost, the hungry, the confused and the tired, and I say to each one of you: read this work repeatedly until you fully understand, while keeping in mind that these small books are certainly no substitute for a "real bible!"

The exclamation marks throughout this work represent my love, passion, devotion and enthusiasm to reach all who are in need of help through *God's "real truth" from a "real bible!"*

Read this work, digest it, sleep on it, understand it and then *you* decide if this theory is fact or fiction, real or imagined!

Acknowledgement

I thank my great-grandmother for sharing with me a "real bible" (when I was a young girl) so that I would have a clear understanding of the difference between God's Word and man's word or the difference between old bibles and *new* bibles or the difference between God's Word and *false doctrine*!

At the time, I am sure, that she was unaware of how she would affect my life, as well as how she would affect the lives of so many through the work that I now share with you.

While deception did exist in the late eighteen hundreds and early nineteen hundreds (when our great-grandparents were born) it did not exist in the magnitude with which it exists today!

Now, if you wonder what I am talking about: I am referring to the more truthful bibles read by our ancestors in years past.

You know! The bibles with the articles and particles! The bibles with "thou" and "knowest" and "thinkest" etc!

You know! The bibles that we have been told repeatedly are too hard for us to read and many have so foolishly believed it and then repeated this to everyone they knew!

The end-result of this deception is that we now live in a world where one does not know the difference between God's Word and false doctrine! Can you imagine? It is time to wake up!

This is what happens to the innocent and unsuspecting when not understanding the deception of our wicked world!

The bibles of our ancestors have been replaced with *many* so-called newer versions where most of the "meat" (truth) of the bible has been removed!

Oops! How dare I write the truth!

This is why I study with "only" the King James 1611 Companion Bible with 198 Appendixes as well as with a Standard King James version, including both old and new testaments.

You might want to check out your bible before you buy it, especially so, if it begins with the word *"New!"*

Take the "meaty" scriptures from this book: Those that reference the anti-Christ, Satan or where God is *against* those that teach his people to fly to save their souls and compare the same scripture; book, chapter and verse to your bible. Are they exact?

This is also why, when working for Our Lord through these small books, I share with the reader, the reference material used. This way, the reader can challenge anything written and look it up for verification.

Why? To determine if what I write is fact or fiction!

Why? I have nothing to hide! This work is about *truth* so why not share the materials used?

So, to my great grandmother and to all the great-grandmothers of the baby-boom generation (or biblically speaking, fig tree generation), I send a sincere and heartfelt thank you for your fantastic contribution to the *truth* that is left in our changing world!

The Ten Commandments

I	Thou shalt have no other gods before me
II	Thou shalt not worship any graven image
III	Thou shalt not take the name of the Lord thy God in vain
IV	Remember the Sabbath day to keep it holy
V	Honour thy father and thy mother
VI	Thou shalt do no murder (to lie in wait)
VII	Thou shalt not commit adultery
VIII	Thou shalt not steal
IX	Thou shalt not bear false witness (lie)
X	Thou shalt not covet thy neighbours house, wife, nor anything that is thy neighbors

Rapture

What is this theory and why is it so important?

It appears that most people, including faithful church goers are unaware that we are in the end-times of this earth age.

They are unaware that the antichrist (Satan) will come to earth first, (before Jesus Christ) to deceive the whole world into thinking he is Jesus.

Many church goers are taught that they don't need to understand the bible because we will all be gone before the destruction of this earth age, because Our Lord will rapture (fly) them out of here!

Well friends, the information I will share with you is too important, for you to not know! So I will do my best to bring you the truth and nothing but the truth, so help me God!

When a loved one dies, we have all heard that she or he is in a much better place, haven't we?

1

This is because our ancestors read more truthful bibles, so they had a much deeper understanding of God's Word than the generations of today and were able to pass this information on.

So let's see if this work can clear up the confusion regarding God's Word and the rapture theory.

Recently, someone put some information in my mailbox on the rapture. They underlined many phrases, and added many stars next to phrases for closer scrutiny.

While this work made reference to many of the books, chapters and versus of the bible it did not quote any of them entirely but did share fragments.

It became quite apparent to me, rather quickly that Our Lord wants you to have the truth once and for all so I will take this very passionate work and *dissect* it, which at this time, I have no idea where it will take me or what the end-result will be but I can't wait!

Consider the Two Bodies

Understand this one thing: We were created with two bodies. We have our flesh body and our spirit body and as soon as the flesh dies it goes back to the dust and the spirit returns to our Father.

1Cor 15:39 All flesh is not the same flesh; but there is one kind of flesh of men, another flesh of beasts, another of fishes and another of birds.

1Cor 15:40 There are also celestial bodies and bodies terrestrial; but the glory of the celestial is one and the glory of the terrestrial is another.

I have looked up some words in the Greek and Hebrew dictionaries indicating the number of the word from the Strong's Concordance.[1]

celestial 2032 above the sky, in heaven, air, sky, to take up or away.[2]   This is the spirit body!

To take up or away? Interesting!

3

terrestrial 1919 worldly, earthly, earth, ground, land, world.[3]   This is the flesh body!

Mt 26:41   Watch and pray, that ye enter not into temptation: the *spirit* indeed is willing, but the *flesh* is weak.

Lk 24:39   Behold my hands and my feet, that it is I myself: handle me and see: for a *spirit hath not flesh and bones*, as ye see me have.

1Cor 15:35   But some man will say, How are the dead *raised up*? And with what body do they come?

1Cor 15:44   It is sown a natural body; *it is raised a spiritual body*.   There is a natural body and there is a spiritual body.

1Cor 15:12   Now if Christ be preached that he rose from the dead, how say some among you that there is no resurrection of the dead?

1Cor 15:13   But if there be no resurrection of the dead, then is Christ not risen?

Now, Our Lord already told us that men would ask how the dead are raised up and in what body. But He also gave us the answer!

We have two bodies, the celestial (spirit) and terrestrial (flesh) and our flesh bodies cannot inherit the kingdom of God!

1Cor 15:50 Now this I say, brethren, that *flesh and blood cannot inherit* the kingdom of God; neither doth corruption inherit incorruption.

1Cor 15:51 Behold, I shew you a mystery; We shall not all sleep, but we shall all be *changed*.

This means we shall not all die (sleep).

1Cor 15:52 In a moment, in the twinkling of an eye, at the last trump: for the trumpet shall sound and the dead shall be *raised incorruptible* and we shall be *changed*.

At the last trump (which is the seventh), we will be changed into our spirit bodies and then raised!

1Cor 15:53 For this corruptible must put on *incorruption* and this mortal must put on *immortality*.

Let's look at the definitions from the Greek or Hebrew dictionaries for these body types.

Corruptible 5349 decayed, perishable, shrivel, wither, spoil[4] - This is the flesh!

Incorruptible 861 unending existence, immortality[5] -This is the spirit!

Mortal 2349 liable to die, to die, be dead, die[6] - This is the flesh!

Immortal 110 deathlessness[7] - This is spirit!

Flesh 4561 human being, carnal, flesh[8]

Spirit 4151 a current of air, breath[9]

Consider the False Prophet

Mt 24:24   For there shall arise false Christs and *false prophets* and shall shew great signs and wonders; insomuch that if it were possible, they shall *deceive* the very elect.

2Cor 11:13   For such are *false apostles*, deceitful workers, transforming themselves into the apostles of Christ.

Prov 14:5 A faithful witness will not lie; but a false witness will utter lies.

Titus 2:10   Not purloining, but shewing all good fidelity; that they may adorn the doctrine of God our Saviour in all things.

Purloining   3557   to   sequestrate,   for   oneself, embezzle, keep back[10]

What are false apostles, false prophets, false witnesses or false Christ's?

7

They are misguided servants (or teachers) of our Lord who think they are doing the Lord's work, but instead are pushing false doctrine which is the same as doing the work of the antichrist!

God hates false oath and false doctrine!

God's word is *not* a matter of individual interpretation! 2Peter 1:20 Knowing this first, that no prophecy of the scripture is of any private interpretation. 2Peter 1:21 For the prophecy came not in old time by the will of man: but holy men of God spake as they were moved by the Holy Ghost.

Jn 5:39 Search the scriptures; for in them ye think ye have eternal life: and they are they which testify of me.

Mt 7:7 Ask and it shall be given you, seek and ye shall find, knock and it shall be opened unto you.

Mt 7:8 For every one that asketh, receiveth and he that seeketh findeth and to him that knocketh it shall be opened.

Rom 16:16 Salute one another with an holy kiss. The churches of Christ salute you.

Rom 16:17 Now I beseech you, brethren, mark them which cause divisions and offences contrary to the doctrine which ye have learned and avoid them.

Rom 1:18 For they that are such serve not our Lord Jesus Christ, but their own belly and by good words and fair speeches deceive the hearts of the simple.

God wants us to know, they lie and they are fakes!

He told us to *mark them* and to *avoid them*!

The clarity of God's Word is just so refreshing and I am grateful to Him for having me bring this work to you!

These are the words of Jesus Christ:

Mt 10:40 He that receiveth you receiveth me and he that receiveth me receiveth him that sent me.

9

Eph 4:13 Till we all come in the unity of the faith and of the knowledge of the Son of God, unto a perfect man, unto the measure of the stature of the fullness of Christ.

Eph 4:14 That we henceforth be no more children, tossed to and fro and carried about with every wind of doctrine, by the sleight of men and cunning craftiness, whereby they lie in wait to deceive.

Eph 4:15 But speaking the truth in love, may grow up into him in all things, which is the head, even Christ.

Need more proof?

Jer 29:8 For thus saith the Lord of hosts, the God of Israel, Let not your prophets and your diviners, that be in the midst of you, deceive you, neither hearken to your dreams which ye cause to be dreamed.

Jer 29:9 For they prophesy falsely unto you in my name: I have not sent them, saith the Lord.

The Dissection

Everything in blue ink is supposed to support the rapture theory according to the writer of the work found in my mailbox.

All text in black is what Our Lord really said to us through scripture, or what I have to say.

The writer states that the following verses are identified with this event.

John 14:3 "Received unto the Lord,"
What scripture really says is:

John 14:3 And if I go and prepare a place for you, I will come again and *receive you unto myself*; that where I am, there ye may be also.

1Thes 4:16 "Caught up to meet the Lord in the air,"
What scripture really says is:

1Thes 4:16   For the Lord himself shall descend from heaven with a shout, with the voice of the archangel and with the trump of God; and *the dead in Christ shall rise first*:

The dead in Christ are those who are dead and gone already. Be sure to repent and ask God to forgive you for not always putting Him first!

Ex: Lk 15:24 For this my son was dead and is alive again: he was lost and is found. And they began to be merry.

2Thes 2:1   "Gathered together with the Lord," What scripture really says is:

2Thes 2:1   Now we beseech you, brethren, by the coming of our Lord Jesus Christ and by our *gathering together unto him.*

There is nothing here about a catching away or being caught up; just that we gather back to Christ.

Although there is no quote for 1Cor 14:33, they say that this scripture clearly states that it is not God who is behind all of the confusion surrounding religion and therefore, it is Satan, our adversary.

Wonderful! We agree! This is the scripture that declares this:

1Cor 14:33   For God is not the author of confusion, but of peace, as in all churches of the saints.

This work says that Satan has always used scripture out of context to have his way or to prevent God's children from knowing the truth.

Who does Satan work through? Man! Which man? The Kenites and the Tares! The heathen, the misguided or misinformed or uninformed!

They quote this scripture as saying:

Jn 8:32 "You shall know the truth and the truth shall make you free," **When this scripture really says:**

Jn 8:32 *And ye* shall know the truth and the truth shall make you free.

Okay, this scripture is close, but my dad always said that close only counts in horse shoes!

This work states that in Matthew chapter four, Satan would use scripture out of context, in his attempt to confuse Jesus.

Mt 4:1 Then was Jesus led up of the spirit into the wilderness to be tempted of the devil.

Mt 4:3 And when the tempter came to him he said, if thou be the Son of God, command that these stones be made bread.

Mt 4:4 But he answered and said, It is written, Man shall not live by bread alone, but by every word that proceedeth out of the mouth of God.

Mt 4:7   Jesus said unto him, It is written again, Thou shalt not tempt the Lord thy God.

Mt 4:8   Again, the devil taketh him up into an exceeding high mountain and sheweth him all the kingdoms of the world and the glory of them;

Then, Satan speaking:

Mt 4:9   And saith unto him, All these things will I give thee, if thou wilt fall down and worship me.

Mt 4:10   Then saith Jesus unto him, Get thee hence, Satan: for it is written Thou shalt worship the Lord thy God and him only shalt thou serve.

There is nothing out of context here!   Satan is toying with Jesus. He's playing games with Him.

When reading a bible that our ancestors read, the scriptures are the same today as they were one hundred years ago. They don't change and do not need to be rewritten! Not now! Not ever!

One could only believe that Satan took scripture out of context because one does not read "God's Word."

This is the difference between reading one of man's books and the Word of God and when one understands the difference and sticks with God's Word only, the confusion disappears.

Now was Satan toying with Our Lord? Absolutely! However, Our Lord put an end to it just like that!

Now guess what? We have the power to do the same! Now how fabulous is that?

This work on the rapture says that there are seven "catching aways" so let's start with the first:

Now the writer only referenced Genesis 5 and no scriptural verse, so let's see what I can find. The catching away of Enoch in Genesis five and two versus in Hebrews were referenced:

Gen 5:24 And Enoch walked with God: and he was not; *for God took him.*

Heb 11:5 By faith Enoch was *translated* that he should not see death; and was not found, because God had *translated him*: for before his *translation* he had this testimony, that he pleased God.

Heb 11:6 But without faith, it is impossible to please him: for he that *cometh to God* must believe that he is and that he is a rewarder of them that diligently seek him.

Okay, now! In Genesis five, I read all the scriptures and didn't find anything that said "catching away." No, not even one!

Now, was the author referring to where "*God took him*?" Or, where Enoch didn't die but was *translated*? Or, was he referring to those who *cometh to God*? Darned if I know!

Now the scriptures tell us that Enoch did not die but that God translated him and *took him* because he was so pleased with him. God *took him* in his spirit body only. Okay!

Translated 3346 In the Greek dictionary means transfer or transport, change sides[11]

All those who have died, have returned to our Father (the spirit that is) and in Enoch's case, he did not die but his spirit left the body and God took him.

The bible tells us that to be absent from this body is to be present with the Lord in:

2Cor 5:6   Therefore we are always confident, knowing that, whilst we are at *home in the body*, we are absent from the Lord:

2Cor 5:8 We are confident, I say and willing rather to be absent from the body and to be present with the Lord.

While in our flesh body, we cannot see the Lord. We need to be in the same dimension as He is to see Him. The dimension being that of the spirit!

Okay, this is easy to understand!

There is still nothing in any of the scriptures in Genesis five about a "catching away." Now, rather than write all thirty two of them, I just put the one that they were possibly referencing.

If you don't have one, you can always borrow a *real* bible and read the entire chapter for yourself! Because I was curious as to what the writer had to say, I looked up every scripture he referenced. It is okay to question people! And you should!

Think about it! This is how mankind got into trouble in the first place! By following man!

Many go to church for an hour a week listening to false doctrine and they think they are following God! God is against false oath! They have listened to and believed all the junk written by mankind which has taken them far away from the truth written within the pages of a real bible!

Now the second "catching away" according to this work, involves Elijah where we are referred to:

2Kings 2:1 And it came to pass, when the Lord would *take up* Elijah into heaven by a whirlwind, that Elijah went with Elisha from Gilgal.

2Kings 2:11 And it came to pass, as they still went on and talked that, behold, there appeared a chariot of fire and horses of fire and parted them both asunder: and Elijah *went up* by a whirlwind into heaven.

2Kings 2:16 And they said unto him, Behold now, there be with thy servants fifty strong men; let them go, we pray thee, and seek thy master: lest peradventure the Spirit of the Lord hath *taken him up* and cast him upon some mountain or into some valley. And he said, Ye shall not send.

There is nothing here about a catching away either! Now the scriptures do say, *take up, went up and hath taken him up* but this is not surprising. Why? The flesh goes back to the dust and the spirit returns to our Father. It is that simple!

Gen 2:7 And the Lord God formed man of the dust of the ground and breathed into his nostrils the breath of life; and man became a living soul.

Gen 3:19 In the sweat of thy face shalt thou eat bread, till thou return unto the ground; for out of it wast thou taken: for dust, thou art and unto dust shalt thou return.

Eccl 12:7 Then shall the dust return to the earth as it was; and the spirit shall return unto God who gave it.

Remember? We came from dust and to dust we return? The spirit came from God and returns to God! We are sown a natural body, we are raised a spirit body!

And again, how are the dead raised up?

1Cor 15:35 But some man will say, How are the dead *raised up*? And with what body do they come?

1Cor 15:44 It is sown a natural body; *it is raised a spiritual body*. There is a natural body and there is a spiritual body.

Now relative to the spirit, read again these scriptures!

2Cor 5:6 Therefore we are always confident, knowing that, whilst we are at home in the body, we are absent from the Lord:

2Cor 5:8 We are confident, I say and willing rather to be absent from the body and to be present with the Lord.

God could not be any clearer! Our body is raised a spirit body!

This work says that the third event is the *taking up* of our Lord Jesus Christ in Acts, chapter 1, so let's see what is said here:

Acts 1:2 Until the day in which he was *taken up*, after that he through the Holy Ghost had given commandments unto the apostles whom he had chosen;

Acts 1:9 And when he had spoken these things, while they beheld, he was *taken up*; and a cloud received him out of their sight.

Acts 1:10 And while they looked stedfastly toward heaven as *he went up*, behold two men stood by them in white apparel;

Acts 1:11 Which also said, Ye men of Galilee, why stand ye gazing up into heaven? This same Jesus, which is *taken up* from you into heaven, shall so come in like manner as ye have seen him go into heaven.

Acts 1:22 Beginning from the baptism of John, unto that same day that he was *taken up* from us, must one be ordained to be a witness with us of his resurrection.

As you can see, the book of Acts, (chapter one) has several references (five) relative to Jesus being *taken up* by Our Father.

I believe the next two scriptures put this to rest.

1Cor 15:12 Now if Christ be preached that he rose from the dead, how say some among you that there is no resurrection of the dead?

1Cor 15:13 But if there be no resurrection of the dead, then is Christ not risen?

God's word is pretty self explanatory!

This work refers to the fourth catching away in the book of John 14:3 and in Romans 5:9, Colossians 3:4 and Thessalonians 1:10 and 4:16-4:18.

John 14:3 And if I go and prepare a place for you, I will come again and *receive you* unto myself; that where I am, there ye may be also.

Rom 5:9 Much more then being now justified by his blood, we shall be saved from wrath through him.

Although Rom 5:9 is a beautiful scripture and their work says that it is a "catching away," you can see that what is claimed is not here!

Col 3:4 When Christ, who is our life, shall appear, then shall ye also appear with him in glory.

Yes, we shall appear with Him in glory, in our spirit body because we will all be changed at the last trump (the seventh)!

1Thes 1:10 And to wait for his Son from heaven, whom he *raised from the dead*, even Jesus, which delivered us from the wrath to come.

1Thes 4:16 For the Lord himself shall descend from heaven with a shout, with the voice of the archangel and with the trump of God: and the dead in Christ shall rise first:

1Cor 15:52 In a moment, in the twinkling of an eye, at the last trump: for the trumpet shall sound and the dead shall be *raised incorruptible* and we shall be *changed*.

You will find the preceding scripture, as well as a few others, in this work more than once because I feel that this is the best way to really drive home the message, so please bear with me.

Now the writer's work states that the scriptures they reference indicate the resurrection and catching away of all the righteous to meet Jesus in the air in the following scriptures.

1Thes 4:17   Then we which are alive and remain shall be *caught up* together with them in the clouds to meet the Lord in the air: and so shall we ever be with the Lord.

1Thes 4:18   Wherefore comfort one another with these words.

I do not see how it would be possible that you could not understand the preceding scriptures with all the information that I shared with you up to this point!

Although the writer claims that a thorough study of scripture proves that all the righteous are gone before the tribulation, he does not provide even one word of evidence to support this!

Why?   Because it does not exist!   Oh my!   How easily we are deceived?

He further states that this rapture must occur prior to the beginning of the tribulation **(persecution, trouble)**, which is a massive act of God's wrath. Interesting!

Now let's remember: To be absent from this body is to be present with the Lord! And also: We are sown a natural body and raised a spirit body!

Okay, he now claims that Genesis five will prove that all the righteous are removed before God's wrath begins so let's see what we have here!

Gen 6:5 And God saw that the wickedness of man was great in the earth and that every imagination of the thoughts of his was only evil continually.

Gen 6:7 And the Lord said, I will destroy man whom I have created from the face of the earth; both man and beast and the creeping thing and the fowls of the air; for it repenteth me that I have made them.

28

Gen 6:11   The earth also was corrupt before God and the earth was filled with violence.

Gen 6:12   And God looked upon the earth and behold, it was corrupt; for all flesh had corrupted his way upon the earth.

Gen 6:13 And God said unto Noah, The end of all flesh is come before me; for the earth is filled with violence through them; and behold, I will destroy them with the earth.

"I will destroy them with the earth!" No confusion here! This is quite clear!

Now, this is what God had to say to Noah and yes, He was angry! He had Noah build the ark, take two of every flesh and two of every kind, male and female. What do you think happened to everyone else who was not on the ark? Gone! Gone! Gone!

Gen 6:19 And of every living thing of all flesh, two of every sort shalt thou bring into the ark, to keep them alive with thee, they shall be male and female.

There is no scripture in the bible that said God completely removed all of the righteous before the flood! So who removed them? No one!

Now this is very interesting, that this person would reference Genesis nineteen.

Two angels went to warn Lot and his family, to get them out of Sodom before God destroyed the towns of Sodom and Gomorrah as well as the people in those towns. Why? Homosexuality!

Why? Abraham appealed to God not to destroy the righteous with the wicked; and there was only this one man (Lot) and his wife and two daughters who were saved from the destruction. His daughters were married but his two son-in-laws did not make it! Why? Homosexuality!

Gen 19:15 And when the morning arose, then the angels hastened Lot, saying, Arise, take thy wife and thy two daughters, which are here; lest thou be consumed in the iniquity of the city.

Gen 19:28   And he looked toward Sodom and Gomorrah and toward all the land of the plain and beheld and lo, the smoke of the country went up as the smoke of a furnace.

In response to the writer's claim that God has always provided for the complete removal of the righteous before an act of His wrath, I must say that in the above case, Lot and his family were spared because Abraham appealed to the Lord *on their behalf* and guess what?   There were only three people out of these towns!

Why?   Too many sins and no one repented?

Who will appeal to the Lord on our behalf?

Now, if God always provides for the complete removal of the righteous, is that writer saying that all who lost their lives in Katrina, the Tsunami or so many other weather related disasters, were not righteous people or God would have removed them?

Who is in control of the weather? God!

There is not, nor will there ever be, a scripture in the bible that states that God will remove completely all the righteous before an act of his wrath! It is not there! It never will be!

You see; mankind prefers to call these occurrences "natural disasters" or "mother nature" at work, while explaining them away with science. When in fact, prophecy is being fulfilled! Big difference!

Who is mother nature? Or mother earth? God! Mmmm! Could God be a woman?

This person references Exodus 14, however no scriptures were given, where evidently, God once again removed all the righteous. Wrong!

Ex 14:10 And when Pharaoh drew nigh, the children of Israel lifted up their eyes and behold, the Egyptians marched after them; and they were sore afraid and the children of Israel cried out unto the Lord.

Ex 14:16 But lift thou up thy rod and stretch out thine hand over the sea and divide it and the children of Israel shall go on dry ground through the midst of the sea.

Ex 14:21 And Moses stretched out his hand over the sea and the Lord caused the sea to go back by a strong east wind all that night and made the sea dry land and the waters were divided.

Ex 14:22 And the children of Israel went into the midst of the sea upon the dry ground and the waters were a wall unto them on their right hand and on their left.

Ex 14:23 And the Egyptians pursued and went in after them to the midst of the sea, even all Pharaoh's horses, his chariots and his horsemen.

Ex 14:27 And Moses stretched forth his hand over the sea and the sea returned to his strength when the morning appeared and the Egyptians fled against it and the Lord overthrew the Egyptians in the midst of the sea.

Ex 14:28 And the waters returned and covered the chariots and the horsemen and all the host of Pharaoh that came into the sea after them; there remained not so much as one of them.

Now, were the preceding scriptures, God removing the righteous, before an act of His wrath? No! Not at all! But rather, it was the deliverance of the children of Israel from the bondage of the Egyptians!

The parting of the sea is biblical and this is how the Lord delivered His children from the hands of the Egyptians! This is the reason we celebrate Passover (not easter)! Big difference!

Ex 1:13 And the Egyptians made the children of Israel to serve with rigour:

34

Ex 1:14 And they made their lives bitter with hard bondage, in mortar and in brick and in all manner of service in the field: all their service, wherein they made them serve, was with rigour.

Ex 1:22 And Pharaoh charged all his people saying; Every son that is born ye shall cast into the river and every daughter ye shall save alive.

Ex 2:23 And it came to pass in process of time that the king of Egypt died and the children of Israel sighed by reason of the bondage and they cried and their cry came up unto God by reason of the bondage.

Ex 2:25 And God looked upon the children of Israel and God had respect unto them.

By the way, do you know who the righteous are? Those who put God first in their lives and those who repent!

Now, **although** this work references the following scripture, there is nothing here about a catching away nor is there anything about God removing the righteous before spilling His wrath either!

Nahum 1:2 God is jealous and the Lord revengeth; the Lord revengeth and is furious; the Lord will take vengeance on his adversaries and he reserveth wrath for his enemies.

Although the above scripture does say that God reserves wrath for His enemies, there is nothing to say He will remove the righteous beforehand, to get them out of the way.

Nahum 1:7 The Lord is good, a strong hold in the day of trouble; and he knoweth them that trust in him.

This work refers to the following scriptures to substantiate removal of the righteous without any quotes so let's see what is said:

1Thes 5:9 For God hath not appointed us to wrath, but to obtain salvation by our Lord Jesus Christ.

Now, who is the "us" here? It is the anointed, the elect, those with the seal, those without spot, those who repent and come back to Him, those who have not been deceived by false doctrine (thereby worshiping the antichrist) and those who put God first in their lives and love Him enough to diligently seek him!

In essence, the "us" are those who have their names written in the "book of life!" The righteous!

Yes, this is biblical! Yes, it can be proven in God's Word! So here it is!

Rev 3:5 He that overcometh, the same shall be clothed in white raiment; and I will not blot out his name out of the book of life, but I will confess his name before my Father and before his angels.

Rev 13:8 And all that dwell upon the earth shall worship *him*, whose names are not written in the book of life of the Lamb slain from the foundation of the world.

The "him" here, refers to Satan and we are told through scripture that "all" will worship him except for those who follow the Lamb, who is Jesus Christ, which is this doctrine that I share with you!

Rev 21:27 And there shall in no wise enter into it any thing that defileth, neither whatsoever worketh abomination or maketh a lie: but they which are written in the Lamb's book of life.

Are you part of this group? Do you know and understand why we are here and what we are suppose to be doing so that you may have your name in the book of life to enjoy everlasting life?

Our Lord and Savior would like all of us to repent and to come back to Him! He wants us to know His doctrine (God's doctrine)! This doctrine!

1Thes 5:9 For God hath not appointed us to wrath, but to obtain salvation by our Lord Jesus Christ.

1Thes 5:10 Who died for us that, whether we wake or sleep, we should live together with him.

1Thes 5:11 Wherefore comfort yourselves together and edify one another, even as also ye do.

The three preceding scriptures from Thessalonians are supposed to firmly establish, once again, the *catching away* of the righteous prior to the beginning of the Tribulation. Wrong! Wrong! Wrong!

I know how to read! I am sure that you know how to read and guess what? It just is not there!

The catching away number five is; according to the misguided writer's work:

Rev 7:9   After this I beheld and lo, a great multitude, which no man could number, of all nations and kindreds and people and tongues, stood before the throne and before the Lamb, clothed with white robes and palms in their hands;

Well! Where is it? It is just not here! That is not suprising! Now, is it?

The catching away number six according to the misguided writer is;

Rev 14:1 And I looked and lo, a lamb stood on the mount Sion and with him an hundred forty and four thousand, having his Father's name written in their foreheads.

Rev 14:2 And I heard a voice from heaven, as the voice of many waters and as the voice of a great thunder and I heard the voice of harpers harping with their harps:

Rev 14:3   And they sung as it were a new song before the throne and before the four beasts and the elders and no man could learn that song but the hundred and forty and four thousand which were redeemed from the earth.

Rev 14:4   These are they which were not defiled with women; for they are virgins. These are they which follow the Lamb whithersoever he goeth. These were redeemed from among men, being the firstfruits unto God and to the Lamb.

Rev 14:5   And in their mouth was found no guile; for they are without fault before the throne of God.

This is the group that is in the book of life!

They made reference to the above scriptures, however, what they claim, just is not here once again! Have you noticed? The only thing the misguided writer got right is that God is not the author of confusion!

Now what is here; is that this is the group that God is pleased with! These are the righteous. If you go back a few pages this is the "us" group!

Do you think that perhaps, this writer was relying on the fact that no one would challenge what he wrote? Or do you think that he didn't expect anyone to take the time to look up every single scripture that he referenced?

According to this person's work the final, being the seventh catching away is the two witnesses of Revelation:

Rev 11:3 And I will give power unto my two witnesses and they shall prophesy a thousand, two hundred and threescore days, clothed in sackcloth.

Rev 11:5 And if any man will hurt them, fire proceedeth out of their mouth and devoureth their enemies and if any man will hurt them, he must in this manner be killed.

Rev 11:6 These have power to shut heaven, that it rain not in the days of their prophecy and have power over waters to turn them to blood and to smite the earth with all plagues, as often as they will.

Rev 11:7 And when they shall have finished their testimony, the beast that ascendeth out of the bottomless pit shall make war against them and shall overcome them and kill them.

Rev 11:9 And they of the people and kindreds and tongues and nations shall see their dead bodies three days and an half and shall not suffer their dead bodies to be put in graves.

Rev 11:11 And after three days and an half the Spirit of life from God entered into them and they stood upon their feet; and great fear fell upon them which saw them.

The misguided writer's work states that after three and a half days of lying dead, the two witnesses are resurrected on camera! Oh, really? Even though that is not in the bible, it is probably something that we can expect from the media today!

Oops! There I go again!

Now, when it happens, remember; prophecy must come to pass and there is no need to be confused because we have been foretold all things.

Mk 13:23 But take ye heed; behold, I have foretold you all things.

When is Jesus coming? According to their work, the answer "is" found in these scriptures. So let us see what this chapter is about.

John 17:1 These words spake Jesus and lifted up his eyes to heaven and said, Father the hour is come; glorify thy Son that thy Son also may glorify thee:

John 17:2 As thou hast given him power over all flesh, that he should give eternal life to as many as thou hast given him.

John 17:4 I have glorified thee on the earth: I have finished the work which thou gavest me to do.

John 17:6 I have manifested thy name unto the men which thou gavest me out of the world: thine they were and thou gavest them me; and they have kept thy word.

John 17:8 For I have given unto them the words which thou gavest me; and they have received them and have known surely that I came out from thee and they have believed that thou didst send me.

John 17:9 I pray for them: I pray not for the world, but for them which thou hast given me; for they are thine.

John 17:11 And now I am no more in the world, but these are in the world and I come to thee, Holy Father, keep through thine own name those whom thou hast given me, that they may be one as we are.

John 17:12 While I was with them in the world, I kept them in thy name; those that thou gavest me I have kept and none of them is lost, but the son of perdition; that the scripture might be fulfilled.

Who is the son of perdition? The only one sentenced to death by name! Yes! He is none other than Satan, the serpent, the devil, the dragon, Baal and many other biblical names including the antichrist!

John 17:15 I pray not that thou shouldest take them out of the world, but that thou shouldest keep them from the evil.

John 17:16 They are not of the world, even as I am not of the world.

John 17:20 Neither pray I for these alone, but for them also which shall believe on me through their word;

John 17:21 That they all may be one; as thou Father art in me and I in thee, that they also may be one in us: that the world may believe that thou hast sent me.

Okay! Mmmm! I do not see here, where Jesus is coming. Do you? By now, this should not surprise you!

Now, what I do read is Jesus talking about the children that God gave Him, and that He lost none and that He kept them in the Word when He was with them!

This person's work closes with; we, as Christians are to get to know one another and have wonderful fellowship and their important clue to when Jesus will return "can" be found in:

Mt 24:44 Therefore be ye also ready; for in such an hour as ye think not the Son of man cometh.

Mt 24:45 Who then is a faithful and wise servant, whom his lord hath made ruler over his household to give them meat in due season?

Mt 24:46 Blessed is that servant whom his master, when he comes, will find him so doing.

When scripture really says lord and not master.

Mt 24:46 Blessed is that servant, whom his lord when he cometh shall find so doing.

Mt 24:47 Verily I say unto you, That he shall make him ruler over all his goods.

I must be missing something! Do you see this "important clue?" Well, I certainly do not! Why? Because it is not there! Oh my! What a shock!

The writer's work states that all we are to do is get along with fellow Christians and bring the lost back to Our Lord.

Phil 1:5 For your fellowship in the gospel for the first day until now.

Phil 1:17 But the other of love, knowing that I am set for the defence of the gospel.

However, there is much more to it than that: We were told to preach the gospel and avoid false oath because God hates it!

2Cor 10:16 To preach the gospel in the regions beyond you, and not to boast in another man's line of things made ready to our hand.

Gal 2:5 To whom we gave place by subjection, no, not for an hour that the truth of the gospel might continue with you.

Lk 13:3 I tell you, Nay: but except ye repent, ye shall all likewise perish.

We are to love our enemies:

Mt 5:44   But I say unto you, Love your enemies, bless them that curse you, do good to them that hate you and pray for them which despitefully use you and persecute you:

We are to love our neighbors:

Rom 13:12   For this, Thou shalt not commit adultery, Thou shalt not kill, Thou shalt not steal, Thou shalt not bear false witness, Thou shalt not covet and if there be any other commandment, it is briefly comprehended in this saying, namely, Thou shalt love thy neighbour as thyself.

Rev 1:3   Blessed is he that readeth and they that hear the words of this prophecy and keep those things which are written therein: for the time is at hand.

The misguided writer said that a rule of theology is not to take scripture out of context and then continues on saying that this rule is violated repeatedly by sincere teachers.

Think about this! Students of religion, (theology majors) cannot possibly know what scriptures say unless they study from God's Word and obviously, the misguided writer does not. This is evident throughout his work!

The writer also said to allow God's Word to speak in context for itself and I believe that I have done that repeatedly.

The writer does not say what book he reads to pull this information but I know for a fact, that the book used, would not meet with the standards of my great-grandmother, nor does it meet with mine!

A summary of biblical phrases; was this writer's definition of the word "rapture."

Please tell me, this writer is not referring to figures of speech; being "seventh heaven" and "cloud nine." If the deception behind this rapture theory was not so sad, this would almost be comical!

I believe there are times when God wants our attention and times when He demands our attention and I am so thankful that He demanded my attention so that I could bring this work to you!

Jn 15:16 Ye have not chosen me, but I have chosen you and ordained you, that ye should go and bring forth fruit and that your fruit should remain that whatsoever ye shall ask of the Father in my name, he may give it to you.

Jn 15:17 These things I command you, that ye love one another.

Jn 15:18 If the world hate you, ye know that it hated me before it hated you.

2Pet 3:3 Knowing this first, that there shall come in the *last days* scoffers, walking after their own lusts.

2Pet 3:7 But the heavens and the earth, which are now, by the same word are kept in store, reserved unto fire against the day of judgment and perdition of ungodly men.

2Pet 3:9 The Lord is not slack concerning his promise, as some men count slackness, but is longsuffering to us-ward, not willing that any should perish, but that all should come to repentance.

Longsuffering 3114 have (long) patience, be patient, patiently endure[12]

Eccl 12:13 Let us hear the conclusion of the whole matter: Fear God and keep His commandments, for this is the whole duty of man.

Eccl 12:14 For God shall bring every work into judgment, with every secret thing, whether it be good or whether it be evil.

This work tells us to be ready because we don't know the day and hour of the appearing of our Lord Jesus Christ and they reference Acts chapter 1.

The appearing of our Lord and Savior is not what we need to be concerned with but to embrace and look forward to, yes! But not to be concerned with!

Acts 1:7 And he said unto them, It is not for you to know the times or the seasons which the Father hath put in his own power.

Acts 1:8 But ye shall receive power, after that the Holy Ghost is come upon you and ye shall be *witnesses* unto me both in Jerusalem and in all Judaea and in Samaria and unto the uttermost part of the earth.

Okay, the Lord is telling us that we are not to know the times or the seasons but he is also telling us that the Holy Ghost which is the Holy Spirit shall come upon us and we will be *witnesses* for Him.

Witnesses for What? When? Where? Why? And against Who?

Well, if we are to be *witnesses* for God, certainly we have to go against someone for God!

The writer probably studies theology (which changes the scriptures) and then passes this on to his readers as truth. It is not! The deceptions of mankind are many and he certainly has been deceived by studying and believing false doctrine.

It is sad to say, but this is the end-result when not studying God's Word? Not to mention that dictionaries help! Yes, the Greek and Hebrew dictionaries to determine the meaning of words beginning with the types of bodies.

1Cor 15:52 In a moment, in the twinkling of an eye, at the last trump; for the trumpet shall sound and the dead shall be raised incorruptible and we shall be changed.

It can't get much easier than this! At the "last trump" we will be changed and then raised up! What is the last trump? The seventh! What happens in the last trump? That is when our Lord and Savior, Jesus Christ returns!

Collectively, in the bible we have been told thousands of times about the wickedness, deception, lies and evil in the world. Additionally, we have been told plenty about our enemies, the liars, the scoffers and those who will persecute us for sharing God's Word but we can take it!

The basis for this writers work appears to be two things: The supposed "catching aways" and the fact that God removes all of the righteous before an act of wrath. Wrong on both accounts! So wrong!

Zec 8:17 And let none of you imagine evil in your hearts against his neighbour; and *love no false oath*; for all these are things that I hate, saith the Lord.

Rev 2:26 And he that overcometh and keepeth my works unto the end, to him will I give power over the nations:

Our God hates false oath and promises power to those who keep his works unto the end! Of course, His works is the "real truth from a real bible!"

Lk 12:1 In the mean time, when there were gathered together an innumerable multitude of people, insomuch that they trode one upon another, he began to say unto his disciples first of all, *Beware ye of the leaven of the Pharisees, which is hypocrisy.*

Mt 16:6 Then Jesus said unto them, take heed and beware of the leaven of the Pharisees and of the Sadducees.

Beware of hypocrisy (leaven)!

Hypocrisy – 2612 / 5272 deceit, wickedness, moral filth[13]

What do you think? Moral filth! Oh my! This is a pretty strong definition, now, isn't it? I just love bold and blunt! Why? No room whatsoever for misunderstanding!

I think these are emphatic warnings because false oath or false doctrine is wickedness, pure and simple!

Where does wickedness come from? Satan and his offspring and or his followers!

Now remember; we obtain salvation through repentance directly to God! Not to a man! This is so emphatically important!

Regardless of how good we may try to be, we are all sinners!

Now, don't forget that only two things follow us into the eternity; our sins not repented for and the work that we have done for Our Lord. Then we receive blessings or chastisement, whichever we deserve.

Why All the Confusion?

Now, if you are wondering why all the fuss? Why all the babble? Why all the confusion?

Let me share why! Clearly and succinctly from God's Word!

Although we are not to know the day or hour that Jesus will return, we can have a deeper understanding of God's word by studying.

Mt 24:36 But of that day and hour knoweth no man, no, not the angels of heaven, but my Father only.

Mt 24:42 Watch therefore: for ye know not what hour your Lord doth come.

Mt 24:50 The lord of that servant shall come in a day when he looketh not for him and in an hour that he is not aware of.

Mk 13:32 But of that day and that hour knoweth no man, no, not the angels which are in heaven, neither the Son, but the Father.

Lk 12:39 And this know, that if the Goodman of the house had known what hour the thief would come, he would have watched and not have suffered his house to be broken through.

Lk 12:40 Be ye therefore ready also; for the Son of man cometh at an hour when ye think not.

Lk 12:46 The lord of that servant will come in a day when he looketh not for him and at an hour when he is not aware and will cut him in sunder and will appoint him his portion with the unbelievers.

Rev 3:3 Remember therefore how thou hast received and heard and hold fast and repent. If therefore thou shalt not watch, I will come on thee as a thief and thou shalt not know what hour I will come upon thee.

Rev 3:5 He that overcometh, the same shall be clothed in white raiment; and I will not blot out his name out of the book of life, but I will confess his name before my Father and before his angels.

You might want to reread the preceding scriptures because most of the world will not be watching for Our Lord and Savior Jesus Christ to return. Why?

Because they will believe that Jesus is already here! Why? Because the media is going to have a field day convincing "everyone" that it is Jesus that has returned, when in fact, it will be the antichrist!

You will want to read the entire chapter thirteen in the book of Revelation but I will share with you some of the scriptures to support what I am saying.

Rev 13:3 And I saw one of his heads, as it were wounded to death; and his deadly wound was healed and all the world wondered after the beast.

Rev 13:8 And all that dwell upon the earth shall worship him, whose names are not written in the book of life of the Lamb slain from the foundation of the world.

You see, God knew thousands of years ago that all (with some exceptions) would worship Satan. Why? Biblical illiteracy!

Rev 13:13 And he doeth great wonders, so that he maketh fire come down from heaven on the earth in the sight of men.

Rev 13:14 And deceiveth them that dwell on the earth by the means of those miracles which he had power to do in the sight of the beast; saying to them that dwell on the earth, that they should make an image to the beast, which had the wound by a sword and did live.

Satan is supernatural and has the power to perform miracles in the sight of men and he will deceive all who are not studying the Word of God!

Rev 13:16 And he causeth all, both small and great, rich and poor, free and bond to receive a mark in their right hand or in their foreheads:

The mark is not a physical mark. If the people are deceived into following the antichrist, the mark is in their mind and if they are doing or supporting the work of the antichrist the mark is in their hand.

Rev 13:17 And that no man might buy or sell, save he that had the mark or the name of the beast, or the number of his name.

There will be a five month period where we will not be able to buy food nor anything, unless we join Satan's one world system, whereby, we will be agreeing to worship him instead of God.

Rev 13:18 Here is wisdom. Let him that hath understanding count the number of the beast: for it is the number of a man and his number is Six hundred threescore and six.

What is threescore? Three times twenty, therefore, Satan's number is 666!

This is the sixth seal, the sixth trump and sixth vial!

I share this information not to frighten you but to help prepare you. We do not need to become hoarders but we do need to plan and prepare for a five month period!

Rev 9:4 And it was commanded them that they should not hurt the grass of the earth, neither any green thing, neither any tree; but only those men which have not the seal of God in their foreheads.

Rev 9:5 And to them it was given that they should not kill them, but that they should be tormented five months and their torment was as the torment of a scorpion, when he striketh a man.

Being tormented by Satan's people is the price we pay for biblical illiteracy! Unfortunately, this statement comes from one who knows first hand!

Definitions

Now, let's see what the dictionaries have to say about these words; I am going to look these words up two ways for you.

The *first* is through the *thesaurus* in my *computer*, which is several years old.

The *second* definition for each word comes from Webster's *dictionary* copyright 1983.

Now let's see what we can find!

1-Theology: religion, divinity, religious studies, spirituality, mysticism and holiness.

2-Theology: The field of study, thought and analysis which treats of God, His attributes and His relations to the universe; the science or study of divine things or religious truth; – a particular form, system, branch or course of this science or study

Okay, these two are similar, however, the first (the thesaurus) does not mention God even once and the Webster's refers to God three times: once with the word God and twice referring to God as His. Webster's also mentions religious truth, while the thesaurus just says religious studies. The thesaurus says mysticism! Yeah right!

1-Religion: faith, belief, creed, religious conviction

2-Religion: Concern over what exists beyond the visible world, differentiated from philosophy in that it operates through faith or intuition and generally including the idea of the existence of a single being, a group of beings, an eternal principle or a transcendent spiritual entity that has created the world, that governs it, that controls it

Remember Genesis 1:1 In the beginning God created the heaven and the earth! It does not say that he had help!

Okay, they both use the words faith and belief, however, certainly, Webster's gives a much deeper meaning although, inaccurate! You will see why in a moment.

Remember the sixth day creation?

Gen 1:27 So God created man in his own image, in the image of God created he him; male and female created he them.

Now what ever happened to evolution? Guess what folks? It is junk! Pure untruth! Total deception!

Remember! Don't talk about religion or politics! It is not too difficult to figure out why now is it? Most of us don't or didn't know what the bible said!

1-Religious: spiritual, devout, sacred, holy

2-Religious: pertaining to or concerned with religion, devout, Godly, a religious man, scrupulously faithful

67

These two definitions share the word devout, however, Webster's, once again uses the word Godly while the computer's thesaurus does not.

Now the Webster's has no problem mentioning the word Christian or Christians, repeatedly, whereas, my computer's thesaurus does not. No, not even once so far, nor does it mention the word God, until one looks up the word God!

1-God - deity, spirit, divinity, supernatural being, idol

2-God - The one Supreme Being, the creator and ruler of the universe!

Oh my! What a beautiful, definition in the Webster's! I much prefer Webster's definition!

1-Idol - icon, hero, statue, god, deity,

2-Idol - An image or other material object representing a deity to which religious worship is addressed. Bible. An image of a deity other than God. Any person or thing devotedly or excessively admired.

Interesting! The computer has god (with a small g), idol and deity being one in the same, whereas, the Webster's has an idol being, other than God!

1-Deity - divinity, god, goddess, idol, divine being, holy being

2-Deity - A God or Goddess, divine character or nature, The character or nature of the Supreme Being, The deity of Christ.

How long did it take you to clearly see the difference between the older and newer work of mankind?

Christ, Christian or Christianity - These words are not even in my computer's thesaurus, however, they are in Webster's as follows:

Christ – Jesus of Nazareth, held by Christians to be the fulfillment of a prophecy in the Old Testament regarding the coming of a Messiah.

Christian - Of pertaining to, or derived from Jesus Christ or His teachings; belonging to the religion based on the teachings of Jesus Christ;

When looking up the word Christian in the Strong's Concordance the definition is;

5546 Christian – followers of Christ[14]

There is nothing here about religion nor will there ever be. Now let me show you why!

The word religion is used in the bible "only" five times and the definitions from the Greek dictionary in the Strong's Concordance are as follows:

Religion 2354 – from 2355 to bewail, lament, mourn 2355 wailing, lamentation, 2360 to wail, clamor, frighten, trouble![15]

Religion   2356   –   ceremonial   observance,
worshiping, 2357 ceremonious worship, pious 2360
to wail, to clamour, to frighten – trouble![16]

In all five instances, in the bible, the word religion
means trouble! Yes trouble!

Mankind   created   all   of   the   denominational
religions!   Yes!   Confusion!   Confusion!
Confusion!   Now, according to our Lord means:
Trouble! Trouble! Trouble! They are experts at
confusion, trouble and deception! Wake up!

I would like the message here to be clear. With the
computer's thesaurus being the newer work and the
dictionary being the older work it is not difficult to
see that biblical truth was removed from the
computer's thesaurus much more so than from the
dictionary.

Now, didn't you think the dictionary's definitions were looking pretty good until I looked up the word religion in the Strong's Concordance?[17] Although I much preferred the Webster's definitions for a while, it just goes to show how much has been lost from the original translations from the Greek and Hebrew languages.

Puzzled? Don't be! Each time there is a translation, more truth disappears! Now, although this is true of the many bibles written, it is also true of the many concordances so be careful. This is why we have been told so many times by our Father about the deception of the world. He foretold us all things! Remember?

The newer the work, the less truthful and the older the work, the more truthful! However, A wise person knows that there are always exceptions!

The sad thing is that many people actually read all the so-called religious work written by men and hold onto it as being truth. It is not! Rely on God's Word for truth!

72

Now that you have the difference between the work stored in my computer's thesaurus and the dictionary, understand this: Christianity is a way of life and *is not* a religion. Why? Religion means trouble! It doesn't get much clearer than that!

Acts 11:26 And when he found him, he brought him unto Antioch. And it came to pass that a whole year they assembled themselves with the church and taught much people. And the disciples were called Christians first in Antioch.

The disciples were called Christians! What is a Christian? Followers of Christ! Who are the followers of Christ? Those who study God's Word!

1Pet 4:16 Yet if any man suffer as a Christian, let him not be ashamed; but let him glorify God on this behalf.

Do you know that recently, my daughter and I went to a "very large, well known bookstore" to buy her a real bible and guess what? There were probably two hundred or more so-called bibles on the shelves. Yes, that many! But guess what? Do you think we could find one real bible? NO! We could not!

So we got into the car and drove across town to a well established store that sells so-called religious items and guess what?

Their bookshelves were full! Yes, full of everything that people had to say and there was not even one book that we could find that had anything at all to say about God's Word! There was also not even one "real" bible on their shelves!

Does this tell you something? Well it should! It is time to wake up friends!

There has always been wickedness in the world but remember; it will all come to an end with one third of God's children following Satan. Why? Because God is going to destroy this earth age!

When friends and acquaintances heard that I was studying the bible, many suggested I read everything under the sun. It appeared as though they would prefer I read anything except the bible. Imagine!

Well, I found myself responding with, "What man (no gender) has to say these days, doesn't really much interest me anymore!" And I meant it! At present, my mission is to help others. The Word of God is the best counselor or medicine that our world has to offer!

I use the Strong's Exhaustive Concordance[18] as a study tool. It is an index to the bible and is the result of the work the Sopherim did.

If you asked me how many times the words deceit, deceitful, deceitfully, deceitfulness, deceits, deceivableness, deceive, deceiver, deceivers, deceiveth, deceiving and deceivings were used, collectively in the bible, I could tell you with confidence, one hundred and twenty five times (unless, of course, I counted wrong)!

Now, if you asked me how many times (collectively) words such as evil, liar, lying, wickedness, thieves, not to mention all that we have been told about adulterers, whores (men and women) and especially our enemies. I could tell you, with certainty, hundreds of times!

Now, if you asked me how many times *any* word was used in the bible, I could tell you, also, but it doesn't end there.

I could also tell you every single book, chapter and verse that any and every word is used in, in the bible as well.

Now, how incredible is that? Do you think that God wants us to understand the vastness of the lies and deceptions in the world? He had the entire bible indexed for us!

God did not put us on this earth to have a good time, nor did He put us here so we could muddle our way through life, messing things up along the way but rather God created us for His pleasure!

Rev 4:11 Thou art worthy, O Lord to receive glory and honour and power: for thou hast created all things and for thy pleasure they are and were created.

Additionally, we are here for two other reasons. We are here to determine if we will follow God or Satan. This earth age is a test! Then, we are to continue the work of our Lord and Savior, Jesus Christ by sharing His Word with others.

Now, let's put aside everything we have *heard or read* and let's truly connect with our own God given gift of common sense!

Study with the bibles read by our ancestors and study with a pastor who will teach word for word from this bible and then and only then will you be following our God and Lord and Savior, Jesus Christ and not man! Remember the "us" group!

The passionate misguided writer was wrong almost entirely. In fact, the only time he was accurate was when he said that God is not the author of confusion but of peace.

At times, he mentioned fragments of scripture that did not align with God's Word, which would cause one to draw the unmistakable conclusion that this writer does not study with, nor does he pull his information from God's Word.

Although I have been able to repeatedly challenge, with backup, what the scriptures really say, I would like to take this work a step further.

The Unforgivable Sin

Do you remember, earlier, where scripture stated that we will be witnesses for God?

Acts 1:8 But ye shall receive power after that the Holy Ghost is come upon you; and ye shall be witnesses unto Me both in Jerusalem and in all Judea and in Samaria and unto the uttermost part of the earth.

Mk 13:11 But when they shall lead you and deliver you up, take no thought beforehand what ye shall speak, neither do you premeditate; but whatsoever shall be given you in that hour, that speak ye; for it is not ye that speak, but the Holy Ghost.

Many will be delivered up before Satan (Only they won't know it is Satan because the media will convince the world that Jesus has returned) to be a witness for God and the Holy Spirit will speak through them. There is nothing here that is difficult to understand!

We have even been told:

Mt 22:14 For many are called, but few are chosen

All other sins will be forgiven with repentance!

Mk 3:28 Verily I say unto you, All sins shall be forgiven unto the sons of men and blasphemies wherewith soever they shall blaspheme:

The next two scriptures state that the unforgivable sin is not allowing the Holy Spirit to speak through you.

Mk 3:29 But he that shall blaspheme against the Holy Ghost hath never forgiveness, but is in danger of eternal damnation.

Mt 12:31 Wherefore I say unto you, All manner of sin and blasphemy shall be forgiven unto men; but the blasphemy against the Holy Ghost shall not be forgiven unto men.

Consider the Enemy

This is Jesus talking to the scribes and Pharisees.

Jn 812 Then spake Jesus again unto them, saying, I am the light of the world: he that followeth me shall not walk in darkness, but shall have the light of life.

Jn 8:21 Then said Jesus again unto them, I go my way and ye shall seek me and shall die in your sins: whither I go, ye cannot come.

Jn 8:23 And he said unto them, Ye are from beneath, I am from above: ye are of this world, I am not of this world.

Jn 8:24 I said therefore unto you, that ye shall die in your sins: for if ye believe not that I am he, ye shall die in your sins.

Jn 8:31 Then said Jesus to those Jews which believed on him, If ye continue in my word, then are ye my disciples indeed;

Jn 8:32 And ye shall know the truth and the truth shall make you free.

Jesus is speaking to those that claim to be Jews (but are not).

Jn 8:37 I know that ye are Abraham's seed; but ye seek to kill Me because My word hath no place in you.

Jn 8:38 I speak that which I have seen with My Father: and ye do that which ye have seen with your father.

Jn 8:39 They answered and said unto him, Abraham is our father. Jesus saith unto them, If ye were Abraham's children ye would do the works of Abraham.

Jn 8:40 But now ye seek to kill me, a man that hath told you the truth, which I have heard of God; this did not Abraham.

Jn 8:41 Ye do the deeds of your father. Then said they to him, We be not born of fornication; we have one Father even God.

Jn 8:42 If God were your Father ye would love Me; for I proceeded forth and came from God; neither came I of Myself, but He sent Me.

Jn 8:43 Why do ye not understand My speech? Even because ye cannot hear My word.

Jn 8:44 Ye are of your father the devil and the lusts of your father ye will do. He was a murderer from the beginning and abode not in the truth because there is no truth in him. When he speaketh a lie he speaketh of his own: for he is a liar and the father of it.

Jn 8:45 And because I tell you the truth, ye believe me not.

Jn 8:46 Which of you convinceth me of sin? And if I say the truth, why do ye not believe me?

Jn 8:47 He that is of God heareth God's words: ye therefore hear them not, because ye are not of God.

Okay, the devil has children living on earth among us! Now this explains a lot doesn't it? Of course, there is so much more information in the bible to support this fact but I will give you just a little more!

Mt 23:31 Wherefore ye be witnesses unto yourselves, that ye are the children of them which killed the prophets.

Mt 23:32 Fill ye up then the measure of your fathers.

Mt 23:33 Ye serpents, ye generation of vipers, how can ye escape the damnation of hell?

Mt 23:34 Wherefore, behold, I send unto you prophets and wise men and scribes and some of them ye shall kill and crucify and some of them shall ye scourge in your synagogues and persecute them from city to city:

Mt 23:35 That upon you may come all the righteous blood shed upon the earth from the blood of righteous Abel unto the blood of Zacharias, son of Barachias, whom ye slew between the temple and the altar.

I think Our Lord is angry! Yes! He is very angry! Now guess what? The bible is not full of love, love, love, as some would have us believe!

Let's face it! Truth is tough stuff! It is not all syrupy sweet! It is oh, so beautiful! And freeing!

Our Lord has cautioned us repeatedly that the wicked one would be coming! And yes! He will be coming first!

Jn 12:31 Now is the judgment of this world; now shall the prince of this world be cast out.

Jn 14:30 Hereafter I will not talk much with you: for the prince of this world cometh and hath nothing in Me.

Eze 28:18 Thou hast defiled thy sanctuaries by the multitude of thine iniquities, by the iniquity of thy traffick; therefore will I bring forth a fire from the midst of thee, it shall devour thee and I will bring thee to ashes upon the earth in the sight of all them that behold thee.

Eze 28:19 All they that know thee among the people shall be astonished at thee; thou shalt be a terror and never shalt thou be any more.

Okay, we will be witnesses for God against the prince of the world! He is to be cast out and brought to ashes before all who behold him! That is easy to understand, isn't it?

Prince 758 – part of 757 a first (in rank or power) chief (ruler) magistrate, prince, ruler[19]

Prince 757 – to be first (in political rank or power) reign, (rule) over[20]

To be first, means to be first, period!

Now who is the prince of this world? Satan!

Jn 16:8 And when He is come, He will reprove the world of sin and of righteousness and of judgment:

Jn 16:9 Of sin, because they believe not on Me;

Jn 16:10 Of righteousness, because I go to My Father and ye see Me no more;

Jn 16:11 Of judgment, because the prince of this world is judged.

In explaining the parable of the tares, Jesus had this to say:

Mt 13:37 He that soweth the good seed is the Son of man;

Mt 13:38 The field is the world; the good seed are the children of the kingdom; but the tares are the children of the wicked one;

Mt 13:39   The enemy that sowed them is the devil; the harvest is the end of the world and the reapers are the angels.

Mt 13:40   As therefore the tares are gathered and burned in the fire; so shall it be in the end of this world.

The only one sentenced to death by name is the son of perdition, who is none other than Satan himself!

Jn 17:12   While I was with them in the world, I kept them in thy name: those that thou gavest me I have kept and none of them is lost, but the son of perdition; that the scripture might be fulfilled.

2Thes 2:3   Let no man deceive you by any means: for that day shall *not come*, except there come a falling away first and that man of sin be revealed the son of perdition.

Remember, that day shall *not come until* the man of sin be revealed! *First!*

There are two tribulations and don't ever let anyone tell you otherwise!

Mt 24:25 Behold, I have told you before.

Mt 24:26 Wherefore if they shall say unto you, Behold, he is in the desert, go not forth, behold, he is in the secret chambers; believe it not.

Mt 24:27 For as the lightning cometh out of the east and shineth even unto the west, so shall also the coming of the Son of man be.

Mt 24:28 For wheresoever the carcase is, there will the eagles be gathered together.

Mt 24:29 Immediately *after the tribulation* of those days shall the sun be darkened and the moon shall not give her light and the stars shall fall from heaven and the powers of the heavens shall be shaken:

Mt 24:30 *And then* shall appear the sign of the Son of man in heaven and then shall all the tribes of the earth mourn and they shall see the Son of man coming in the clouds of heaven with power and great glory.

When will the Son of man come? *After* the tribulation of those days!

Want more proof?

Mk 13:21 And then if any man shall say to you, Lo, here is Christ, or lo, he is there; believe him not:

Mk 13:22 For false Christs and false prophets shall rise and shall shew signs and wonders, to seduce, if it were possible, even the elect.

Mk 13 23 But take ye heed: behold, I have foretold you all things.

Mk 13:24 But in those days, *after that tribulation*, the sun shall be darkened and the moon shall not give her light,

Mk 13 25 And the stars of heaven shall fall and the powers that are in heaven shall be shaken.

Mk 13:26 *And then* shall they see the Son of man coming in the clouds with great power and glory.

We are told the same thing! If someone tells you Jesus is here, don't believe him! And again! When does the Son of man (Jesus) come? *After* that tribulation!

What does tribulation mean? *2347 afflicted, burdened, trouble*[21]

Jn 16:33 These things I have spoken unto you, that in me ye might have peace. In the world ye shall have tribulation but be of good cheer, I have overcome the world.

Rev 2:10 Fear none of those things which thou shalt suffer; behold, the devil shall cast some of you into prison, that ye may be tried; and ye shall have tribulation ten days: be thou faithful unto death and I will give thee a crown of life.

Mt 10:28 And fear not them which kill the body, but are not able to kill the soul: but rather fear him which is able to destroy both soul and body in hell.

We have been told that Satan comes first!

2 Thess 2:3 Let no man deceive you by any means: for that day shall not come, except there come a falling away first, and that man of sin be revealed, the son of perdition;

2 Thess 22:4 Who opposeth and exalteth himself above all that is called God, or that is worshipped; so that he as God sitteth in the temple of God, shewing himself that he is God.

2 Thess 2:5 Remember ye not, that, when I was yet with you, I told you these things?

Repent

Recently, I was talking with a woman in her seventies, when I asked her if she repents and she replied with: Well, no! I haven't done anything wrong!

When I asked, if she realized that gossip or judging others were terrible sins she said, "Oh, no! I think I have been bad! I think I have been very bad!"

Oh my! She was so honest! How refreshing!

Jer 18:8   If that nation against whom I have pronounced, turn from their evil, I will repent of the evil that I thought to do unto them.

Nation means a large group of people.

Jer 26:3 If so be they will hearken and turn every man from his evil way, that I may repent me of the evil, which I purpose to do unto them because of the evil doings

Jer 26:13 Therefore now amend your ways and your doings and obey the voice of the Lord your God and the Lord will repent him of the evil that he hath pronounced against you.

Jonah 3:9 Who can tell if God will turn and repent and turn away from his fierce anger, that we perish not?

Lk 13:3 I tell you, Nay: but except ye repent, ye shall all likewise perish.

The preceding scripture doesn't say that we might perish if we don't repent! It says we shall all perish if we don't repent!

Is this said to frighten you? Heck no! It is said to help you understand just how little we know about God's Word! Why? We haven't been taught and we don't read!

This was said to help people open their eyes and their minds, so that they may understand there is far more to God's Word than most of us have realized!

94

Eze 14:6 Therefore say unto the house of Israel, Thus saith the Lord God; Repent and turn yourselves from your idols and turn away your faces from all your abominations.

Eze 18:30 Therefore I will judge you, O house of Israel, every one according to his ways, saith the Lord God. Repent and turn yourselves fom all your transgressions; so iniquity shall not be your ruin.

Acts 3:19 Repent ye therefore and be converted that your sins may be blotted out, when the times of refreshing shall come from the presence of the Lord;

2Peter 3:9 The Lord is not slack concerning his promise, as some men count slackness; but is longsuffering to us-ward, not willing that any should perish, but that all should come to repentance.

Longsuffering means patient.

Haven't we been taught that all we had to do was to go to church once a week and occasionally go to confess our sins to a man?

When I was young, this just did not seem right to me! It didn't make any sense that we would share our deepest, darkest secrets with a man!

Although I did not understand then, I certainly do now! We are to repent directly to God and do not need an intercessor (man) between us and Our Living God! How beautiful is that?

Matt 4:17 From that time Jesus began to preach and to say, Repent: for the kingdom of heaven is at hand.

Matt 6:12 And they went out and preached that men should repent.

Matt 6:13 And they cast out many devils and anointed with oil many that were sick and healed them.

Lk 17:3 Take heed to yourselves: If thy brother trespass against thee, rebuke him and if he repent, forgive him

Lk 17:4 And if he trespass against thee seven times in a day and seven times in a day turn again to thee, saying, I repent; thou shalt forgive him.

Acts 17:30 And the times of this ignorance God winked at; but now commandeth all men every where to repent:

Rev 3:19 As many as I love, I rebuke and chasten: be zealous therefore and repent.

Do you think repentance is a must? If not, you may want to reread these scriptures until you understand!

Do you remember, when mankind began with "little white lies are okay?" Well guess what?

There is nothing in the bible that says little white lies are okay! Lies are lies! Period!

I say this because this is just one more of Satan's subtle deceptions!

We are all wretched sinners, regardless of how much we may want to believe that we are good people!

How can I make this statement?

I make this statement with confidence because there are few who know the difference between false doctrine and God's doctrine and I also make this statement because anything we put before God is breaking the first Commandment!

This includes families, homes, cars, television, bank accounts, pets and anything and everything else that you can think of that we put before God!

So I remind you to repent often, because it is oh, so important! If you did not understand before, you should now!

I think you get the picture!

Consider the Feasts of Our Lord

Lev 23:1 And the Lord spake unto Moses, saying,

Lev 23:2 Speak unto the children of Israel and say unto them concerning the feasts of the Lord, which ye shall proclaim to be holy convocations, even these are my feasts.

Lev 23:3 Six days shall work be done: but the seventh day is the sabbath of rest, an holy convocation; ye shall do no work therein: it is the sabbath of the Lord in all your dwellings.

Remember the fourth commandment?

IV Remember the Sabbath day to keep it holy!

Lev 23:4 These are the feasts of the Lord, even holy convocations, which ye shall proclaim in their seasons.

I am not going to share all forty four scriptures with you but I would like to suggest that you read Leviticus 23 entirely.

Read it, study it and remember that God told us to "search the scriptures!"

Regarding all of God's feasts and festivals, we will save that for another book at another time!

Do you remember when our Lord said not to make his Father's house a house of merchandise?

Jn 2:16 And said unto them that sold doves, Take these things hence; make not my Father's house an house of merchandise.

God is against those who have turned His churches into stores of merchandise and businesses!

Why? God's word is not about money! It is about truth! This truth!

Need I say more?

Consider Easter

Did you know that the word "Easter" is used in the bible only one time? Yes, only once, and that scripture reads as follows!

Acts 12:4 And when he had apprehended him, he put him in prison and delivered him to four quaternions of soldiers to keep him, intending after *Easter* to bring him forth to the people.

Now, when looking the word Easter up in the Strong's Concordance;[22] it's definition is as follows:

Easter – 3957 the Passover, (the meal, the day, the festival or special sacrifices connected with it) compare (OT6453) from OT6452; used only techically of the Jewish Passover (the festival or the victim): Passover, offering OT 6452 a primitive root - to hop, skip over[23]

Skip over how? To the side of Satan! If you are not on the side of God and His only begotten Son, Jesus Christ, then you are on the side of the devil! Not too hard to understand now is it?

Mt 6:24 No man can serve two masters: for either he will hate the one and love the other, or else he will hold to the one and despise the other.

Now, the Vine's Expository Dictionary of New Testament Words[24] has Easter, 3957 as a *mistranslation* and states that the term Easter is not of Christian origin and was not instituted by Christ.

After the Passover ended, the ungodly continued into the evening with a pagan festival of their own called Easter.

Oh my! Do you think we have been badly deceived? We have been warned repeatedly of the wickedness of the world, as well as false doctrine!

Now, if the word Easter is used in the bible only one time and the word "Passover" is used in the bible seventy six times, which one do you think is really of God, and therefore is Christian?

Which one do you think we should be celebrating?

Now, when looking up the word Passover in the Strong's,[25] we are referred again to *3957 easter, Passover.* However, when looking up the word in the Vine's Expository[26] the definition of Passover is a feast instituted by God in commemoration of the deliverance of the children of Israel from Egypt.

1Cor 5:7 Purge out therefore the old leaven, that ye may be a new lump, as ye ate unleavened. For even Christ our Passover is sacrificed for us:

Christ is our Passover! We are to celebrate Passover and not Easter!

Num 28:16 And in the fourteenth day of the first month is the Passover of the Lord.

Num 28:17 And in the fifteenth day of this month is the feast: seven days shall unleavened bread be eaten.

Lev 23:4 These are the feasts of the Lord, even holy convocations which ye shall proclaim in their seasons.

Lev 23:5 In the fourteenth day of the first month at even is the Lord's Passover.

Eze 45:21 In the first month, in the fourteenth day of the month, ye shall have the Passover, a feast of seven days; unleavened bread shall be eaten.

Lev 23:6 And on the fifteenth day of the same month is the feast of unleavened bread unto the Lord: seven days ye must eat unleavened bread.

Lev 23:7 In the first day ye shall have an holy convocation: ye shall do no servile work therein.

Deut 16:1 Observe the month of Abib and keep the Passover unto the Lord thy God: for in the month of Abib the Lord thy God brought thee forth out of Egypt by night.

What is the month of Abib? It is April! The first month of the year? Now, what do you think of that?

1Cor 5:8 Therefore let us keep the feast, not with old leaven, neither with the leaven of malice and wickedness; but with the unleavened bread of sincerity and truth.

Mt 26:2 Ye know that after two days is the feast of the passover and the Son of man is betrayed to be crucified.

Jn 2:23 Now when he was in Jerusalem at the Passover, in the feast day, many believed in his name, when they saw the miracles which he did.

Jn 12:1 Then Jesus six days before the Passover came to Bethany, where Lazarus was which had been dead, whom he raised from the dead.

105

Jn 13:1 Now before the feast of the Passover, when Jesus knew that his hour was come that he should depart out of this world unto the Father, having loved his own which were in the world, he loved them unto the end.

Certainly, there is much more on the Passover in the bible! However, I believe that I have shared enough information with you to open your eyes!

Christ is our Passover! The highest sabbath day of the year and just take a look at what mankind has done! The price we pay for biblical illiteracy is steep! Very steep!

Do you know that the pig (swine) was not created by God to be eaten by man? Imagine!

Lev 11:2 Speak unto the children of Israel, saying, These are the beasts which ye shall eat among all the beasts that are on the earth.

Lev 11:3   Whatsoever parteth the hoof and is clovenfooted and cheweth the cud, among the beasts, that shall ye eat.

Beast of course, is an animal. Need more?

Lev 11:7 And the swine, though he divide the hoof and be clovenfooted, yet he cheweth not the cud, he is unclean to you.

Lev 11:8 Of their flesh shall ye not eat and their carcase shall ye not touch; they are unclean to you.

Lev 11:46 This is the law of the beasts and of the fowl and of every living creature that moveth in the waters and of every creature that creepeth upon the earth:

Lev 11:47   To make a difference between the unclean and the clean and between the beast that may be eaten and the beast that may not be eaten.

Deut 14:8   And the swine, because it divideth the hoof, yet cheweth not the cud, it is unclean unto you: ye shall not eat of their flesh, nor touch their dead carcase.

We have been given so many warnings, but few were reading the Word of God!

1Tim 4:1   Now the Spirit speaketh expressly, that in the latter times some shall depart from the faith, giving heed to seducing spirits and doctrines of devils;

1Tim 4:2   Speaking lies in hypocrisy, having their conscience seared with a hot iron;

1Tim 4:3   Forbidding to marry and commanding to abstain from meats, which God hath created to be received with thanksgiving of them which believe and know the truth.

God is angry that His people have been deceived by false prophets; believing they can't eat meat on Friday's!

Well guess what? It is not biblical! Abstaining from eating meat on Friday (or on any day) is not in the bible! Oh my! Have we ever been deceived?

Now, according to Our Lord, we were not to abstain from eating meat! Do we see what happens when man follows man? We end up following the ways of the wicked!

1Cor 10:20 But I say, that the things which the Gentiles sacrifice, they sacrifice to devils and not to God: and I would not that ye should have fellowship with devils.

1Cor 10:21 Ye cannot drink the cup of the Lord and the cup of devils: ye cannot be partakers of the Lord's table and of the table of devils.

Jn 3:18 He that believeth on him is not condemned but he that believeth not is condemned already, because he hath not believed in the name of the only begotten Son of God

109

Jn 3:19 And this is the condemnation, that light is come into the world and men loved darkness rather than light, because their deeds were evil.

Jn 3:20 For every one that doeth evil hateth the light, neither cometh to the light, lest his deeds should be reproved.

Jn 3:21 But he that doeth truth cometh to the light, that his deeds may be made manifest, that they are wrought in God.

Jn 3:36 He that believeth on the Son hath everlasting life: and he that believeth not the Son shall not see life; but the wrath of God abideth on him.

Jn 4:23 But the hour cometh and now is when the worshippers shall worship the Father in spirit and in truth: for the Father seeketh such to worship him.

Jn 4:24 God is a Spirit and they that worship him must worship him in spirit and in truth.

Who Will the Enemy Target

Mk 13:20   And except that the Lord had shortened those days, *no flesh should be saved*: but for the elect's sake, whom he hath chosen, he hath shortened the days.

Rev 9:4   And it was commanded them that they should not hurt the grass of the earth, neither any green thing, neither any tree; but only those men which have not the seal of God in their foreheads.

When the bible uses the word men, there is no gender here. It means both men and women.

In Rev 9:4 God told Satan he can hurt anyone he wants who does not have the seal of God in their minds! Which is God's real truth! This truth!

Now, that is why this work, is so important for you to understand! Get rid of the confusion, babble and false doctrine that you have learned once and for all and get into God's word so you will be protected by Him!

111

Rev 9:5 And to them it was given that they should not kill them, but that they should be tormented five months and their torment was as the torment of a scorpion, when he striketh a man.

Rev 9:10 And they had tails like unto scorpions and there were stings in their tails and their power was to hurt men five months.

This five month period is Satan's reign on earth, so that is why it is so important to know and understand this truth!

Do you know that our enemies refer to themselves as ships? One of their phrases used to connect with others who are joining the side of wickedness, is "A rising tide raises all ships!"

If you are wondering what this means, it is that Satan is recruiting so many of God's children to the side of wickedness and refers to the increased wickedness in the world today as rising ships.

112

Interesting?

Well, I will tell you, I pray they enjoy their rising ships now while they have them because where they are going, I would not want to go!

God is going to destroy this earth age because one third of His children will follow Satan instead of God! Let's see, how many billion children is that?

Now guess how they refer to us? They refer to us as the "bewildered herd!" Imagine!

Why is this? It is because they know how easily led people are and how easily deceived and how lazy we are. They think that they, as the rising ships are superior to the humble and unsuspecting, leaving us to wallow in the confusion that they have created!

Well, I have news for them: Pride is what got Satan the death sentence! I pray this prideful group knows what they are doing!

Eze 28:15 Thou wast perfect in thy ways from the day that thou wast created, till iniquity was found in thee.

Iniquity 5766 - evil, iniquity, perverseness, unjust, unrighteousness, wicked, 5765 distort[27]

Eze 28:17 Thine heart was lifted up because of thy beauty, thou hast corrupted thy wisdom by reason of thy brightness; I will cast thee to the ground, I will lay thee before kings, that they may behold thee.

Brightness 3314 – splendor, beauty 3313 to shine[28]

Eze 28:18 Thou hast defiled thy sanctuaries by the multitude of thine iniquities, by the iniquity of thy traffick, therefore will I bring forth a fire from the midst of thee, it shall devour thee and I will bring thee to ashes upon the earth in the sight of all them that behold thee.

Eze 28:19 All they that know thee among the people shall be astonished at thee; thou shalt be a terror and never shalt thou be any more.

Now, who is bewildered? Certainly no one who studies with Shepherd's Chapel! And certainly no one who studies with the bible used by our great-grandmothers!

Now, Satan accomplishes his work through his many recruits. Man is continuously twisting scripture and rewriting "The Word" with their so called easy to read bibles.

They are masters of confusion through their false bibles and false church denominations to confuse mankind so that we won't know what to believe!

Now guess what? It worked! Many still can't see the truth even when they read it! Why? They have been so brainwashed! Do you remember?

Don't talk about religion or politics! Mmmmm! Gee! I wonder why not? Do you get it?

Now, as though there isn't enough confusion, let's bring science into God's Word! Why? More confusion! What is the definition of bewildered? Confusion!

Who is behind all of the confusion? Satan and his offspring and his followers!

It appears to me that man doesn't want to just muddy the water with all of their false teachings and babble but rather, they prefer quick sand to mud!

Now, let me ask you this! They have done a good job with all of this confusion, haven't they? Oh yes, they have! Only they have overlooked one mighty important fact!

Our great-grandparents who read the Word of God from a real bible! And those of us who live and remember!

116

God's word is very clear and concise and does not change from day to day or year to year!

The confusion comes from the antichrist who has his many followers pushing false doctrine and false teachings and false oath with untrue bibles! Those behind this work are God's adversaries (enemies)!

Mt 6:24 No man can serve two masters for either he will hate the one and love the other or else he will hold to the one and despise the other. Ye cannot serve God and mammon (money)!

This could not be any clearer!

Yes, their mission is to kill the souls that should live, and yes, this is biblical!

Eze 13:18 And say, Thus saith the Lord God; Woe to the women that sew pillows to all armholes and make kerchiefs upon the head of every stature to hunt souls! Will ye hunt the souls of my people and will ye save the souls alive that come unto you?

Eze 13:19   And will ye pollute me among my people for handfuls of barley and for pieces of bread to slay the souls that should not die and to save the souls alive that should not live, by your lying to my people that hear your lies?

Eze 13:20   Wherefore thus saith the Lord God; Behold, I am against your pillows, where with ye there hunt the souls to make them fly and I will tear them from your arms and will let the souls go even the souls that ye hunt to make them fly.

The pillows symbolize the covering up of the truth!

I have done my best to share with you enough information so there should be no doubt whatsoever in your mind as to whether this theory is fact or fiction, real or imagined, truth or deception!

Read, read and reread! Yes, until you get it!

We don't absorb by reading only one time so read and reread until this information is embedded in your mind!

In Closing

Jn 16:12 I have yet many things to say unto you, but ye cannot hear them now.

Jn 17:2 As Thou hast given Him power over all flesh, that he should give eternal life to as many as Thou hast given Him.

Jn 17:3 And this is life eternal that they might know Thee the only God and Jesus Christ, Whom Thou hast sent.

Jn 17:4 I have glorified Thee on the earth; I have finished the work which Thou gavest Me to do.

Jn 14:26 But the Comforter, Which is the Holy Ghost, Whom the Father will send in My name and shall teach you all things and bring all things to your remembrance, whatsoever I have said unto you.

Jn 6:35 I am the bread of life: he that cometh to Me shall never hunger; and he that believeth on Me shall never thirst.

Jn 8:12   I am the light of the world; he that followeth Me shall not walk in darkness but shall have the light of life.

Jn 15:16 Ye have not chosen Me, but I have chosen you and ordained you that ye should go and bring forth fruit and that your fruit should remain: that whatsoever ye shall ask of the Father in My name, He may give it you.

Jn 15:17 These things I command you, that ye love one another.

Jn 15:18   If the world hate you, ye know that it hated Me before it hated you.

Jn 15:19 If ye were of the world the world would love his own: but because ye are not of the world, but I have chosen you out of the world, therefore the world hateth you.

Why are we here? So that God may determine who we will follow; God or Satan and so that we may "love one another" by bringing God's truth to others, therefore, helping them to emerge from darkness to light!

This is how Our Lord and Savior intended for us to live and it doesn't get any more beautiful than that!

The intent of this work is to provide you with the facts behind the rapture theory.

If you want truth, get a real bible and if you want a truthful teacher find Shepherd's Chapel!

I use as a reference guide, "The New Strong's Exhaustive Concordance of the Bible." [29] This work includes Greek and Hebrew dictionaries.

Now, if you are wondering why this particular concordance, when there are so many out there; the reason is really quite simply this:

Because I study with a "real bible" like the one that my great-grandmother read and I study with Shepherd's Chapel, which teaches truth from this "real bible", I know that I can trust any product that they carry and sell!

Oh my! Truth and trust, all under one roof! How beautiful is that? What a concept! Is this new!

1Peter 4:17   For the time is come that judgment must begin at the *house of God*: and if it first begin at us, what shall the end be of them that obey not the gospel of God?

There should be no doubt whatsoever in your mind that the "rapture theory" is the greatest lie of all time and is the greatest threat to the salvation of mankind! May God be with you now and always!

Mt 28:20   Teaching them to observe all things whatsoever I have commanded you: and lo, I am with you alway; even unto the end of this world. Amen.

1-29   Used by permission of Thomas Nelson, Inc.

TITLES BY THIS AUTHOR

CONSIDER TRUTH GOD'S TRUTH

CONSIDER EVERY WORD OF
JESUS CHRIST
2 volumes

RAPTURE FACT OR FICTION
YOU DECIDE

CONSIDER THIS BEFORE
HAVING A CHILD

In Research and Development

CONSIDER GOD'S WAY OUT OF
HOMOSEXUALITY

Think about the *truth* within the pages of this book. I learned more in two months of study with this chapel than I did going to church for ten years. Imagine!

To gain further understanding watch Shepherds Chapel daily for thirty days and make up your own mind and I believe you too will reach the same conclusion that I have, which is that this chapel teaches the word of God as God intended His word to be taught!

Call Shepherds Chapel
@ 1 800 643 4645

www.shepherdschapel.com

Call for this free tape (*a must have*) and viewing time in your area!

May God Bless you and your family now and always!